TIME MANAGEMENT

Time Management

How to conduct a conversation

Power Phrases

Decision Making Tools

S. Ramkhelawan

Introduction

This concise book I have written to communicate, to make things easier for everyone. From the very beginning to the present day, the history is propelled by means of communication. This skill is easy to learn for everyone. I hope that this book is a fascinating journey of self discovery for you, by which you understand yourself and in people-to-people relations. About 260 ready-to-use phrases to support your communication are discussed. I hope you enjoy reading and success!

If you want to be succesful, where it concerns mastering your time, you have to act as follows:
1. You should have a plan
2. You should be able to apply some skills
3. You must communicate well with your environment, listen carefully to others, indicate if something goes wrong. It is important that you manage awkward situations by discussing it.

Proper diagnosis is half the cure.

Your time management skills are proper when you:
- Can listen carefully to others
- Can say no or reject proposals
- Give and receive criticism properly
- Ask questions
- Effectively tell what you want
- Communicate well with others

- Are able to manage conflicts
- Delegate
- Are going for win-win negotiations

Time management is the ability to plan and control your time to effectively accomplish your goals.

Chapter 1

Conducting a conversation

Conducting an interview

In any interpersonal contact is most important that the person who asks questions controls the conversation. So, the one who asks questions controls the conversation. Think of your youth, you are also brought up with: "If you are asked a question, answer it." If you ask questions to someone. He answers or feel compelled to respond. Although the other person does not answer, he is at least encouraged to respond. Inwardly, he is already working on the question and the answer to it. He answers the question to himself

For example, let me ask you a question.
If you would win 10 million Euro tomorrow.

What will you do?

What will you buy?

How do you want to spend those 10 million Euro?

Will you keep your job?

Will you donate a part?

You may find that when asking these questions, your thoughts are making huge moves in order to formulate answers immediately.

This is a normal and automatic response of anyone who is asked a question.So when you ask questions, you are the leading factor in a conversation until you in one way or another way get an answer to your question. By asking questions you tackle the other, it is like grabbing his jacket and pull it towards you. Questioning the other holds also his attention.The question is a powerful communication tool and technique to influence issues.

The following types of questions you can use to be more effective in both your business- as well in your personal life. The search for opening opportunities to establish a conversation belongs to skill number one.

Some considerations are:

- ask creative and relevant questions

- apply a novelty or a news message in a talk

- be sincere complimentary

- hook in a previous conversation or experience

1. Open ended questions

These questions start with: who, what, where, when, why and how.

An interesting question that you can ask someone you meet is: "What is your profession?"

This is a nice general question and easy to answer.Everyone is fascinated by his work or career.To some extent, you will receive a response.

If your question is answered, you can continue with: "What has led you to do this?"

Given that everyone is fascinated by his work or career you'll get more details. Keep the conversation going on with questions like: "why did you make that choice, or why is that interesting."

If the conversation starts to expire, not running as expected you can to throw more dynamics in by asking as follows:

"What did you do next or why did you do that." You can keep the conversation going with the previously listed questions in both business and private.
You can also ask other questions such as: Why did you choose that approach? When did you start that particular route? Where do you live?Where are you from?

Open questions require that the other party provides a detailed answer to your questions.That simply cannot be ' yes ' or ' no ' answers.

That is also the approach by asking those questions.The more you ask, the more opportunities you get to listen to the answers.

And the more you are listening to matters that interest them orregard them, as their careers and achievements in the past and the present, the more they will regard you as a good interlocutor, the more receptive they will be for your proposals or ideas.

2. Close ended questions.

These are questions that require a "yes" or "no" answer.The other party must make a choice between the previously given answers. The answer is already built in the question. An example of a close end question is: Do you find satisfaction in your activities? Did you have a nice holiday? Will you reply tomorrow on my request?

As a reminder, I give you two considerations:

- when you start an conversation or would keep a

conversation going on, use open ended questions

- if you want a clear answer or decision use closed ended questions.

3. You can initiate an conversation with a question by building in a suggestion for the answer.An example is: "Uncle Joe, I'd like to go with you to dinner." What suits you best: "Friday or Saturday night."

4. You can also ask questions by which others immediately know where they stand. There exists no doubt about what you want with your question. For example: Are you satisfied with the service?

5. A different, but effective way to find out the opinion of another is by asking indirect questions. He does not recognize the intention of the question. For example: How likely is it that you will recommend a friendto do business with us? In all these cases you are the guiding factor in the conversation as long as the other party has not responded. By asking questions, you will get a better understanding about his thinking, his attitude, his beliefs and his framework. By this you are able to play cards, to make better proposals, to deliver tailor-made proposals for better results.

Let me give you some comments that you can use in a good conversation:

- How was it?

- How is it?

- How should it be?

 - Under what conditions?

 - Under what circumstances?

 - Since when?

Sometimes it is necessary to request more.

This questioning is necessary when you experience as follows

- you get a different answer to your question

- you get an incomplete answer

- you get an unclear answer

- you get an answer which is not relevant

A balanced conversation is one that has a good mix of effective listening, short breaks, asking the right questions and good responses to what the other person is saying or proposing. If the conversation is not running smoothly or you find that you are too much to the word, pause and start the conversation with open ended questions.

What ever the other party says, you stay positive and constructive in your approach. You give no evidence of adverse reactions or feelings. You can agree, yes-nodding, and empathize. For example, say: 'I understand your perception and feelings both but. ....'

A listening ear works wondersFor all individuals you come across there are only two that don't say much:

-those who do not talk much (the silent one)

-those who talk a lot (the programmer)

During the conversation you constantly ask the following questions:

- do I get evidence or are these generalities. Evidence convincesyou better than generalities

- what is the evidence that you are being offered

This can be:

- equations

- statistics

- evidence

- photos

- maps

- charts

- images, etc.

A reliable way to find out whether the facts are right is by getting answers to the who-, what-, where-, when-, why- and how-questions.

Ask yourself constantly these questions :

Where does the story go to?

What is the core of what the other person is saying?

What is the essence of what the other person says?

What is the heart of his argument?

Do you know where you stand?

An interview should never be dominated by speaking

loudly, by speaking quickly or by speaking continuously.

It is like a big gorilla that knocks on the chest and verbally letsknow who has the upper hand.

People go to a counselor, for example, a psychotherapist, to talk about their feelings, experiences or about something that has happened. This has a listening ear and continues to engage constructively whatever the speaker says. In your private atmosphere, you can also be an excellent help by asking questions about:

- how they feel

- how they are doing

and by:

- listening patiently

- not to respond negatively

- not judging

The best gesture that you can create in people-to-people contacts is not to judge. Herewith you present yourself as a powerful and balanced discussion partner. By not judging you will be experienced as a powerful and balanced interlocuter.

A good interlocutor is looking at the other when he speaks with him. He smiles, nods, agrees and speaks words like yes...hmm .... aha, imitates the movements of the other, etcetera.

Observe yourself once you dance with your partner.

You will both have the same moves and have fun.

It is said that dancing is the best seducer!

It is said that sincere attention is the highest form of flattering.

Good communicators:

- have a high degree of empathy with their conversation partners

- are sensitive towards them

- take into account their feelings

They try to move constantly in the interlocutor.

Instead of downplaying their feelings and concerns, they try to imagine how they would feel if they were in their shoes. A powerful way of communicating with someone who has problems or feel uncomfortable is:

- recognize and by saying: 'I understand exactly what you feel, if I were in your place I would feel exactly the same.'

People have the need to feel that others understand and show their sincere empathy with their circumstances or situation. By saying: 'I understand exactly what you feel, if I were in your place I would feel exactly the same' you send a powerful message which people appreciate, respect and make them look up to you.

This makes them more accessible to you.

And this can post better results in the future.

You can influence them better. The most important thing in this is that you build trust by listening to others.

And trust is the basis in all relationships with people.

And all together we are the society.

If someone speaks to you act as follows:

1. Listen carefully listen to the entire conversation without interrupting the speaker. Listen as there is no other speaker in the country, he is the only speaker in the country. Listen and understand every word, nod, say yes, laugh, use expressions like ah ..... hmm .... yes ... You will be amazed at the impact you can have on others by fascinated listening. You will be amazed at the influence you can have on others by listening fascinated.

2. Pause before you speak, as the other party stops talking wait a few seconds before you begin speaking. An indication is approximately 4 seconds. If you pause, you will hear the other person better. The words pronounced by the other will penetrate to you and you will be able to hear him better. This allows you to answer more intelligent than when you, would respond immidiatly. Also notice that you consider his words before you answer. This is very flattering for the speaker. By this you let the other know that what he says is valuable or important to you.

Maybe the other still considering and by pausing you let the other know that you are a good, qualified interlocutor.

3. Ask for clarification

Never assume that everything the other person is saying, trying to say or proposing is clear. Sometimes an answer or question or incomprehensible. Especially when it comes to business talks, where it can involve complex issues, always ask for clarification before starting to answer or display your own approach. Conversely, one does sometimes as if your answer / question is not understood ore makes clear that he does not understand your answer/question. Then stay persistent (without getting angry) and repeat your question.This does require some tact.

Do you have doubts? Then ask: 'How do you mean? ' This is a powerful question to follow a conversation and check it. It is almost impossible not to answer this question.

Do you have doubts? Ask for more information.

Possible approaches to the questions are:

What does that mean?

Tell me more about it

Can you repeat the question?

Could you be more specific?

Repeat the answer please?

Or you say nothing and let the silence work for you, you may receive more information, and then question further.

4. The last is summarizing the answers of the speaker in your own words. You can say, 'Let's see if I have understood you.' 'What you say is this ' and then summarize in your own words. This shows you that you pay attention to what the speaker says and endeavouring to understand him well. By doing so, others will feel comfortable in your area, they feel appreciated.

By listening your goodwill and confidence grows. This listening also strengthens the self-respect and self-esteem of the speaker.

Key principles that can help are:

That's interesting, tell me more.

That's interesting, why do you say that?

That's interesting, why are you doing that?

That's interesting, why do you ask that?

By listening you grow goodwill and trust.

The speaker or attach your resume or he will explain it again.

Be alert to the person who summarizes you put any words in your mouth. He must show your statements correctly.

Never feel the pressure to respond positively / straight into a meeting or conversation. One of the strong tools that you have at your disposal, is taking time to think. You can perfect build relationships with others, by asking good questions and by listening to people.

Summary

Look the other person in the conversation.

Ask questions to clarify what is being said.

Show interest by asking also about the feelings of the other.

Repeat some parts of the conversation.

Put above all no pressure on the other.

Stay quiet and calm.

Smile and and nod yes.

Stay alert.

Do not attack the other

Interrupt correctly.

Note

Note

_____

_____

_____

_____

_____

_____

_____

_____

Note

_____

_____

_____

_____

_____

_____

_____

_____

Chapter 2

PHRASES

Below I present a number of phrases to support your communication. You can get them in single or combined.

Remember, confronting the other party with circumstances or facts can be very useful, but be careful with this; you should both come true.

1. Ask who-, what-, where-, when-, wh-y, and how questions. Why questions are particularly suitable, they also have something philosophical. Philosophers are drilled and trained in asking the why question.

2. We should not deal with imperfections from the past, let's focus on the future.

3. You give only one side of the case. You should also do it from the other side.

4. If someone makes good comments to what you are saying, and you do not want to get involved, you can say: "That's a good starting point, I will think about it."

5. One can neutralize a reason for resistance, by exaggerating, by downplaying. One can negate the resistance by emphasizing own positive items.

6. Those arguments are far-fetched.

7. If someone launches a plan, analyze the total plan view with which points suits you, Those points one must be emphasized and the others just do not talk about it.

8. Sometimes use the rhetorical question and do not respond to challenges. A rhetorical question supposes, that the other party agrees to what the transmitter (speaker) suggests.

For example:

"Do you still care?"

"Do you still want to earn a lot of money later?"

9. Sometimes you can say on an offer/proposal:

Too late and too much.

Too late and too little.

Too early and too little.

Too early and too much.

10. Is someone coming with a bad example, one can say. "This is an isolated case, an example of what should not be done." and then emphasize the positive points of the majority.

11. I am assuming that everyone aids by the agreements.

12. I have said this to you and, you still are asking why? "Because we might be too critical." "We must ask ourselves whether we can handle all of this."

13. The issue has left quite a bit of annoyance and disappointment.

14. During a conversation, Let see what you all did to make a positive impression. In order to strengthen that you can sometimes also mention the negative points of the other part. "I am of good will, that is my style of negotiation; I approach things from a positive attitude, that testifies my entire career."

15. If someone asks a question see if it is a question or a packaged convicted.

16. I can not change the agreement anymore but I still can make reservations.

17. Giving up privacy is the hardest thing there is.

18. My words are differently explained. My statements are taken out of context.

19. In a hard attack strike back hard or one can say: "I'm a little used to it. I can take away from there. "

20. At first there were some misunderstandings, there was perhaps talk of mutual incomprehension.

21. Sometimes you can say: "I'm going to take this or that step"and later perspective with: "that was a possibility."

22. In the case of threats, difficult negotiations, one breaks, stalling the other party. Think about a strategy.

23. Sometimes you can attack someone better with one word than wirh 10 ideas.

24. It's better in difficult topics to be an entertaining person and avoid to make exact statements.

25. Traditionally, it is unsympathetic that the good suffer under some evils.

26. The most difficult problem to overcome is the problem that we do not see. If we do not see that something is a problem, we come not on the idea to do something about it.

27. The last time you were serious and uncertain. But you are definitely not on your friend.

28. Sometimes does someone have a disturbed relationship with the truth.

29. With each agreement; How do you check that the agreements also be complied with?

30. I have listened to your conversation with increasing amazement. I sincerely believe that there is a large, gaping misunderstanding

31. Do you know how he thinks? "Yes, but I am not going to tell you. "

32. I believe in your good intentions, but I'm afraid that..................

33. That is at least a little lucky situation.

34. Understanding is something else than to agree.

35. Why have you not mentioned this before? "Because we had underestimated the problem."

36. What will you do? "I don't know yet, I'm going to see what can not and what should not .

37. What has moved you to do that? It gives us problems. "It was a desperate act."

38. The individual ignorance is only partly to solve. Persons concerned must also take note of the information.

39. If someone proposes something you don't agree with, you can say: "I wish you good luck with your intention."

40. In case of problems, lay everything out and say: "What can you do for me?"

41. I have acted in good faith on the information, that was given to me by the Secretariat.

42. I want a major satisfaction it is not about the money.

43. If you quote someone quotes, quote him the right wayand correctly.

44. By quoting select one can prove everything.

45. We do not live in the fear of the next attack round. But developing own opinions about task and future as much as possible ahead of time.

46. We need to work together and don't blame on each other. If we do not change the current situation there is no future for us.

47. It is not just a question of childishness or jealousy, but also a sense of insecurity.

48. I consider this to be a victory of the common sense.

49. The word trick does not belong to us, but in the circus.

50. That is an intorable question. I'm not a Crone walking behind everything jam.

51. If someone says: "you are here to answer the questions one can say: "But you have no right to silence me, I should tell my story too. "

52. It is only human that people forget or deny some things.

53. I could not get rid of my story.

54. What are you doing?

How is it going?

Is it the truth?

Have we done everything we could?

Are there things we could not handle?

55. Sometimes a hard pronunciation is necessary to stop a discussion

56. I have no explanation for what happened.

57. About officials and aid workers. Do they do their job well or properly? Do they fit our laws on the right way?

58. If someone says: "I think this or that about you, or something with you to do " you can answer as follows: "So, you think that that is true?"

59. His decisions are completely the opposite in comparison

with all previous insurances that he has done regarding this matter since...........

60. During a negotiation there is a tendency to overcharging.

61. Why do you talk about this and not about that? Answer: "because I can't talk about everything at once."

62. It is not about people, but about the policy conducted.

63. If someone first make good comments about you and afterwards attacks you, you can say: "Are you confused?"

64. Sometimes there is reason to respond in a way that the other does not expect. Think of the journey of Anwar Sadat to Israel.

65. Regret speaking out is all too easy when it comes to words which anyone could have thought.

66. In provocative comments can you say: "I assume he has such tantalizing statements to stimulate the discussion. "

67. What is it: "perjury or a difference of interpretation?"

68. Precisely because of the research he had understood that in good faith, errors were made.

69. Keep expectations of a discussion low, you can post easy say that the results are good.

70. It was an appointment with a responsible, for

example, an official, who was competent to act so.

71. Sometimes one seizes external influences to cover internal failure.

72. Your attitude says a lot about the intentions you have regarding the decisions to be made.

73. I have no explanation for what has happened.

74. What is leadership?
That's to determine guidelines in the company and send it to the people, so they have clarity about what should and what should not. Leadership also means dealing with signals (feedback) from the staff/stakeholders regarding directives that you send.

75. You will when delivering criticism have to take into consideration some limits of the realities that also count for the opposing team, opposition.

76. We are satisfied with what has been achieved after lengthy discussions regarding the trip, the delegation, representation, etc.

77. If unexpected party is chosen. "I didn't have asked that clarity, which is more or less provided to me. That clarifies the matter."

78. In dealing with people.

How to give them the idea that you appreciate them.

How do you pretend that they contribute, even though they sometimes have none.

79. As a consequence of the program delays and budget overruns, there is a liquidity problem. A strengthening of equity is therefore necessary. On how this should be done is currently under consultation.

80. Sometimes you can, if you don't agree with the results of a thorough research challenge, the procedure or method of examination.

81. If not, clear who has done something, you can say: "I think so slowly that no one did it.But it is shown to have happened.

82. It is almost always true that he who pays, wants to determine what is happening with the money.

83. There is a misunderstanding, and there is indeed a communication disorder from which we get nervous.

84. In asking for help.
Ask or require help? "Would you please" sounds more attractive than, "I want you..................."

85. Sometimes someone is grasping ideas like a nanny. Has lack of creativity, thinking, laziness or lack of fantasy. It then seems like that his current level of knowledge is the highest possible.

86. Our work is unjustly discredited.

87. How shabby you will feel if you unjustly are seen for defaulter.

88. There should be these days a retroactive relief about that action in the past which everyone rejected .

89. You must give a true and fair view of the actual extent of the damage, the unrest, crime, etc.

90. A man is a community being. Please try to deal with others as you would like to be treated yourself.

91. You should always keep your own dignity.

Lose control of yourself?

That can't be right?

You become weak, you will be vulnerable

92. Good fences make good neighbors.

93. The task of the representative is to represent the people to monitor the Government, and together with the Government to make laws. The problems are complicated single advocacy is not possible.

94. Sometimes, one needs to make decisions that do

not correspond to the short term needs of the grassroots.

95. You have to make sure that the reporting, your statements, never conflict with the interests of your organization or your own.

96. Always think of

1. What do I do on my own accord?

2. What do I do in response to what the other person says or does?

97. As long as I am not giving you an answer, you can not even suspect what I am going to reply.

98. Better a living dog than a dead lion.

99. We will try to match your invitation as much as possible with our agenda.

100. If people come here with closed minds, I have no damn chance to convince them? It that case it becomes a nondiscussion.

101. It is always good to think. Thinking never harms.

102. According to the lawyer........ acted unlawfully by declaring that .... (fact)............... that has

not taken place

103. It is good, pending a court case, negotiation, not to make comments.

104. That act is an unacceptable low point.

105. He uses a kind of salami tactics, with each time a piece of security, employment is broken down under the pretext of rationalization, effectiveness and automation.

106. In order to avoid misunderstandings, I wish to declare that with emphasis that stupidity and illiteracy are no synonyms, of which he is a living proof.

107. The law obliges the state its organs and officials to confidentiality about the ins and outs of the citizens and the data of the citizens. Officials/managers are held to secrecy.

108. The facts must be judged objectively by all parties, regardless the private or personal insights

109. I'll give you the opportunity to say: "the state of affairs was not good."

110. If there are apologies that should be offered, it's your turn then.

111. It's nice to hear how the arguments are adjusted.It does not matter what arguments are put

forward. One picks them up just out from anywhere..

112. From a common friend I have learned that I can trust you.

113. He did not want to come, because the invitation was based on the wrong assumption.

114. One of the outcomes was that the stakeholders, who were not satisfied with the product/service, had complained and had gotten any satisfaction, their criticism was ventilated to ten other people.

115. Every person is innocent until his guilt is proven

116. He left due to disagreement about the policy to be pursued.

117. The officials/aid workers should have a helpful attitude in their work regarding citizens and their interests.

118. Your work is making you paranoid, you are up to vacation.

119. Set out your track record without much emphasis. Set out achievements on a wide area and try to push the opponent on the defensive by emphasizing certain behavior now or in the past.

120. He tries to belittle the reporting by saying that there was nothing new in the State.

Note

_____

_____

_____

_____

_____

_____

_____

Note

_____

_____

_____

_____

_____

_____

_____

_____

Note

_____

_____

_____

_____

_____

_____

_____

_____

121. He saw that his words would have no effect.After all, as had the experience learned, particular ideas will not disappear, nor by reasonable arguments nor by wise counsel.

122. In the fierce attack by the counterpart you can say: "I can't help that the counterpart has collapsed.

123. The discussion is very concrete, clear in my view. I don't let others provide me alibis by. They need to take their own decisions.

124. Some reluctance had graced him, if only to avoid the impression that he came to the same questionable level as the others.

125. The judge makes decisions on the basis of evidence that is legitimate and convincing. In their absence, there must be acquitted.

126. My compliments for your sense of duty and dedication.

127. Do no try to convince someone sometimes, just let see what you would do in such a case.

128. However, you have failed adequately to address the human dimension.

129. A lack of inner civilization.

130. Is it true what he says?

So is it and this is how we do it.

131. In the case of a suspicion must be a reasonable suspicion

132. In the case of gossip I see it so differently: "to make it a bit bluntly, if I walk on the street, I know that there are sewers below. But I walk on the street. I don't sit in the sewers ".

133. We don't accuse you and work you not against you. This is

our common analysis, which leads to our conclusion that this is best.

134. Suddenly, without any cause the man threatened me, us, the others under the outbreaks of abject curses.

135. In the post hearing of facts. The fact that there was no openness make that we feel misled. If we had been informed about the facts and not heard by accident or trough others, we would say: "that's over forget it." But now there is a lack of confidence. We do not wat this kind of situations.

136. It occurs to me that you are accustomed to crass statements. That will no doubt have to do with your upbringing.

137. The best navigators are on shore.

"I'm not a navigator."

138. I agree with you, but I was step lower.

139. It is reasonable and fair for all parties contribute a proportional share of the proof or facts.

140. Sometimes the moral has the same size as the wallet.

141. On the basis of my function I demand that.
"You can't reasonably demand that from me."

142. A visitor who is clearly less concerned.

143. An old proverb: "You can use dirty water to put fires out."

144. The aid worker must explain the patient in easy-to-understand language, the disease, prognosis, the treatment method, and the possible side effects.The right of the patient/client should be respected;

He is free to decide on the treatment method.

145. Target of false accusations, blatant lies, and false representation of conviction.

146. Who wants to be everyone's friend is everyone's lackey.

147. You remain receptive, open to others, without loosing your your own interests ; that's what you tell

your fellow man.

148. You don't have to apologize for any other occasion, unless it's a necessity.

149. A tree that knows to bend will not be broken by the wind.

150. We want to highlight the dangers of this development.

151. Social talks are based on equations.

152. If one is faced with direct talks or evidence, one can directly answer with:

When?

Who?

Why?

Ask questions to see if the person concerned is in doubt.

153. Taking the whole situation into consideration, comparingthe opportunities, there would be no support for him. That's why I have taken the decision not to proceed. It would be flogging a dead horse. That comparison is a bit irreverent, but the case is

clear.

154. I give you this as added information, not as an excuse.

155. I don't sit on the same level as you are, therefore I cannot go on with you.

156. A little mucus seems to me more appropriate than threatening with a Court case.

157. If you cooperate with a tort you will have with no doubts limited rights.

158. If one is experiencing something, one searches for security at fellow sufferers.

159. Responsibility is not only to your environment, people, family, but also to yourself. Make sure you do not undermine your own position. You will then be a clown.

160. That stems from frustration.

161. It is brain work, you can't excelerate that.

162. Sometimes you need to look at how it works, what works, rather than how it should be, what it should be.

163. What do you hope? Hope comes from the despair. You should cherish hope. Sometimes against the dismal odds.

164. I do not want a showdown. I don't want to argue with you as an authority.

165. Could you explain to me the actual legal bases on which you that think it can come true?

166. In case of questions or the service could not be better, or the accounting could not be better, etc. Through this kind of questions it shows that it's not good enough. On the way we can make improvements is under discussion now.

167. A man with a right or left philosophical belief.

168. That is sentimental error and as result a big one.

169. It is better to have less well in your familiar environment than to go on adventures in foreign lands.

170. Who has the power, must be humble.

171. The situation has a stormy development recent days.

172. Revenge, even if is that sweet, is not acting with common sense.

173. There is already a formula for solving the problem, but apparently there is very little progress.

174. In a discussion to strengthen your position, you can say: "I don't want to have the last word, but the

core issues, that's what it's about."

175 The result does not meet the expectations.

176. As true as I stand here, I'll submit a protest letter.

177. Party interest takes precedence over loyalty to a person.

178. That reasoning comes from the left wing or liberal wing.

179. For example: there must be a solid and democratic alternative visible.

180. That leads to an inexhaustible source of legitimate protests.

181. In some cases it is necessary to sacrifice a lot in order to preserve everything.

182. Someone on the dock.

183. Do you think that he will grant your request? "If it is up to me sure."

184. It is better that one envies you your luck, then complain about your adversity.

185. You'll be in a deep darkness of trouble if you're not careful.

186. How do you solve that problem? I wonder how.

187. In case of damage: "In comparison with what I could be that not enough."

188. Some objections are wellfounded, another unfounded, but those are for improvement.

189 At criticism "Oh well, fun is different, but it does show that our organization still is democratic and criticism is allowed. And there are you guys for"

190. In some circles the prevailing believers are paternalistic what means: "keep them ignorant and dependent"

191. Initially it was said to me that I was an outsider, had no experience. I have learned quickly. It is also a comment on all subjects against newcomers. If it was the ever lasting thuth there would be never, new young lawyers, notaries, teachers, bank employees or bakers.

192. I have taken note of your point of view. I do not agree with your point of view.

193. How can one resume communication:

1. "Is there anything else you would like to say?"

If no: Well, then, I would like to make a comment.

2. I see that it's difficult to talk for you. Maybe there

is something you can put difficult into words.

3. I don't know what made you stop with that.

I wonder if this is related to what I said.

4. The previous time a silence fell, you said that it had to do with what I had said, had done, or with your experience. Can you tell me more about it?

194. The other party declares that they are still the representative, or still want to talk. "We have told the other party that his attitude during that (.......................) has raised many questions and by this his credibility has been affected. "

195. Borrowing costs, budgetary always more than save.You must only have to a sacrifice in advance

196. Advantage of voluntary work is the added value where the Government can't meet.

197. The latecomer by his performance seems to say: "my time is more important than yours, therefore you can wait until I amfinished."

198. He is accused of that... offence. What I hear let so many possibilities open from serious involvement to total innocence.

199. He had every confidence that the Commission, the Court or his employer would be swayed

200. It is very important that people should know where they stand. The decision making process should be transparent. If decision making is incalculable, this has a crippling effect on the people, especially if they are accustomed to clarity and responsibility. Everything can then stagnate. It works highly demoralising on the organization , the morale drops. Innovation and entrepreneurship are coming under pressure.

201.. Why should I know better?

202. If I want to communicate with the others, seems to me the most appropriate way to do that directly and not through you.

203. You talk about a storm in a teacup. The investigation will prove that I have told the truth; and facts don't lie. I'm not worried.

204. In love and war is not everything goes according to the rules.

205. I hope this action, this request is not lost and that it willachieve its goal and will reach the receivers, attendees.

Note

_____

_____

_____

_____

_____

_____

_____

_____

_____

Note

Note

_____

_____

_____

_____

_____

_____

_____

_____

206. An essential part of our democratic system is the right of self-determination of each member of the community, at least to the extent that the rights of fellow citizens do limit it.

The principle of equality is very important. Equal cases to be treated equal. Unequal unequally

207. If someone says, invoking your feeling. "Do you trust me?" Then you can safely say: "Have you done something causing me not to trust you?"

208.. Why should I know better?

209. If someone sends you a question about a confidential issue, can you say: "That's a question for you but the answer in mine."

210. If you do not want to give the purchase price of something for whatever reason say that is was a bargain.

211. With aggressive questions or objections, ask a quiet why question.

212. If there are to many questions can you say: "I don't need to answer all your questions."

213. If someone keeps asking your opinion to say: "You need to stop getting my opinion, I hope you feel that too."

214. In the case of unexpected questions can you say: "I do not like sneaky questions, please no other question?"

215. If you want to do a proposal , say: "I want to ask you a question to see if you can reach your goals in a constructive manner. Is that good for you? "

216. You will receive a proposal to be involved in something then you can say: "Can I think about it a few days and come with some ideas on how I can help?"

217. In the case of delicate issues one can reply: "We must also be prepared to review this issue from a more psychological side and a creative solution where both parties are happy with."

218. Watch that fair comparisons are made wherever it appears, and if possible, do not apply comparisons.Say: "Let's leave it in my case."

219. That's theoretical. I don't think it will be so

220. When you took office there were many promises, but now it appears to be different; How comes that? It is clear that at the time we were overly optimistic.

221. I don't know how his thought process, but he has a signal.

222. That's theoretical. I don't think it's that.

223. People who make something clear sound hard for us. While they are not at all hard.

224. I am, either directly or indirectly, or tacitly involved.

225. How do you rate it? "I'm not the conscience of the people."

226. If you don't know the answer just say so. Man cannot know everything.

227. I don't hold them on other people's actions.

228. How do you rate it? "I'm not the conscience of the people."

229. we will that change? "That's an idea."

230. He's got a lot of criticism; What do you think of that? Criticism of him partially I agree. But I would use otherwords.

231. Even though I do that I'll keep the one I am. I want life to be more pleasant.

232. I enter everything that is intelligent. That idea of yours draws me not at all, but there are interesting aspects.

233. In a slip, one can say I will review the situation

234. Your own wallet is despite all nice thoughts, still the only by which you must pay.

235. I don't have any frictions with anyone. I only want my rights.

236. This is a hypothetical question and I would ask you the same; that I do not go on in.

237. That's what you are saying is inappropriate.

238. Do you feel misunderstood?
"No, but I also felt not overvalued."

239. I'm not people shy, but I do not like to step off on people.

240. That's at least a little lucky situation.

241. That is a (bad) example of what can happen if not careful

242.I am Hitchkok not?

"That wouldn't be a bad example."

243. Don't you think that as a result, frictions arise?"Is is possible. But that's a challenge for us. "

244. How did that happen? There are different theories about.I don't know.

245. Working with him has an advantage, that I don't have to work with you.

246. What people know about themselves, which makes them afraid.

248. In the case of persistent accusations you can say: "if someone told you those things about me to you, you are brainwashed."

249. He has abandoned you?
"No, he has retreated to think."

250. The limits of the permissible.

251. Sometimes one must be content with insufficient information about the actual state.

252. Some individuals live in the assumption, have the illusion that they enjoy high regard.

253. What happens if you do not agree with each other? "In that case we will help each other where we can."

254. Understanding is anything other than agree.

255. Look you must make no comparisons, but consider the situations on a case-by-case basis. Let's leave it at my case.

256. Deliberate concealment of facts (cheats) is very different from the not fully reveal what you think at some point.

257 If, for example, your adviser comes and says: "if

he gets the majority I will draw back, in that case you must do it yourself."

Depending on the situation this may have two sides. Or he is no longer able to guard your interests or he has other interests and puts you under pressure (blackmail).

258. Do you think that is acting with common sense? You will find that good? You say: "I appreciate your concern for common sense." "I appreciate your concern for the well."

259. By saying that this is your final offer is you can come back to it later with the statement: "it was not my very last bid."

260. In the case of errors or harassment, etc. you can reply with: "that's sloppy and in social or other way can not be tolerated."

261. In times of adversity is the ingenuity of people much bigger than in times of prosperity.

262. In the event of a problem you can lay everything out and ask: what can you do for me?

263. If employees of a company do not have the right attitude and there is a lack of information, that may have consequences for the turnover.

This includes:

- correctness

- manners

- service

Service means no drudgery

264. As a surrogate for internal problems will people choose external threats.

265. We are with two or three parties here, if you want we can all go wrong. So let us work together.

266.. In some comments can you say: "You say so,that means that you have a lot of experience with that."

267.. If you want to interrupt someone you can say: "I was justwondering what you were going to say, when you started talking. Would you say it again? "

Note

_____

_____

_____

_____

_____

_____

_____

Note

Note

_____

_____

_____

_____

_____

_____

_____

_____

Chapter 3

Decision making methods

Decisions are made on the basis of what we see, hear, smell, feel and taste. An example is the test driver of a vehicle that you would like to purchase. There are criteria that determine what decision you take or decision you make meets the criteria.

A decision should not degenerate into: 'I have bought something or I have decided something but I don't know what I'm getting.' That's a adventure that a sane person will not put up with. In making decisions frequency, intensity and duration are important.

Back to the example of the vehicle.

How intense would you use it?

How frequently would you use it?

How long (duration) would you use it?

On the basis of these criteria you convince yourself to make a decision. How often do you think before you decide? There are people that never decide and there that decide fast, intuitive, instinctively or automatically.

I am giving you the following 3 approaches which you can apply when making decisions:

1. The stumbling thread decide method

Always formulate a stumbling thread when taking a decision. For example, before every decision you should take, a week cooling-off period.

2. The walking decide method

Go an hour walking if you want to make a decision. Do you have many doubts after this, then you may safely assume that you do must consider better.

3. The five-to-seven-time-decide-method

This method a method that I employ and which for me always works well. A friend of mine has a business and there is the rule that a wheel bolt must have five to seven strokes before securing. With that in my mind, I start experimenting with the

'five-to-seven-time-decide-method" when taking a decision. I think five to seven times over before I make a decision, convince myself about criteria or by another source. As said before, this is a method that I emply and which for me always works well.

This concise book I have written to communicate, to make things easier for everyone. From the very beginning to the present day, the history is propelled by means of communication. This skill is easy to learn for everyone. I hope that this book is a fascinating journey of self discovery for you, by which you understand yourself and in people-to-people relations. About 260 ready-to-use phrases to support your communication are discussed. I hope you enjoy reading and success!

Note

_____

_____

_____

_____

_____

_____

_____

_____

Note

_____

_____

_____

_____

_____

_____

_____

Note

_____

_____

_____

_____

_____

_____

_____

_____

Note

_____

_____

_____

_____

_____

_____

_____

_____